HEMINGWAY

HEMINGWAY

Nicholas McDowell

Wayland

Life and Works

Jane Austen
The Brontës
Thomas Hardy
Hemingway
D.H. Lawrence
Katherine Mansfield
George Orwell
Shakespeare
H.G. Wells
Virginia Woolf

Cover illustration by David Armitage

First published in 1988 by
Wayland (Publishers) Ltd
61 Western Road, Hove
East Sussex BN3 1JD, England

Series adviser: Dr Cornelia Cook
Series designer: David Armitage
Series editor: Susannah Foreman

British Library Cataloguing in Publication Data

McDowell, Nicholas
    Hemingway. — (Life and works).
    1. Fiction in English. American writers.
    Hemingway, Ernest, 1899–1961
    I. Title   II.Series
    813'.52

ISBN 1–85210–491–0

Typeset by Kalligraphics Ltd, Horley, Surrey
Printed and bound in the UK
By The Bath Press, Avon

Contents

1
Introduction

Ernest Hemingway was born in Oak Park, Illinois, a suburb of Chicago, in 1899 and died in Ketchum, Idaho in 1961. He was one of the greatest American novelists of this century, one of the greatest short story writers of any nation or period. He witnessed three wars, was wounded in the first and wrote a masterpiece about the second.

His best writing often deals with the tragic areas of man's experience, with violent death and lost love, with the struggles of men and women to maintain their dignity in the face of personal crisis and battle.

Hemingway displayed himself to his public as an indomitable hero, a tough guy who had proved himself in war and excelled at dangerous sports. He was a boxer, a big-game hunter, a fanatical fan of bullfighting. Courage under the threat of death, which he sometimes called 'grace under pressure', was the quality that he admired most in others and hoped to stand for in the public eye. Beneath this mask of unconquerable masculinity, Hemingway was a sensitive, deeply troubled man who doubted his powers as a writer, a lover and a fighter. The tension between the public and private man can often be felt in his writing. He spent more time doing battle with the written word and with his own emotions, than in punching, shooting, fishing or soldiering.

It is for the narrative style which he slowly developed and refined during the early part of his career that

Opposite
Hemingway as a bearded war correspondent in Europe. He was present at the Normandy landings in 1944.

Hemingway will be best remembered. This style is so clear, precise and apparently simple that many have thought it easy to imitate. It is not. Under the straightforward surface of Hemingway's prose, complex currents of feeling cross and recross. He created a style of writing that was able to reflect and report the mood of the first part of this century, a time in which old faiths were abandoned and traditional values questioned.

Hemingway was gifted with enthusiasm and curiosity, with a thirst for experience and for alcohol. He married four times and became friends (and, later, enemies) with some of the major literary figures of his time. The sporting vigour that characterized his early years led to accidents and illnesses which depleted his natural energies and his imaginative gift. He used up too much of himself too quickly. For the last years of his life he struggled with depression and, in 1961, convinced that he had destroyed his own ability, he committed suicide, a man lost to himself.

Hemingway's genius lay in his ability to transform his experiences of historical moments and private pain into works of art. He was able to render the personal as universal, to forge out of his own observations stories that spoke to everyone in a style that made his insights available to all. He believed that pain and loss were the necessary ordeals that make a writer. In a letter to the American novelist F. Scott Fitzgerald, written in 1934, Hemingway emphasized this point: 'We are all bitched from the start and you especially have to be hurt like hell before you can write seriously. But when you get the damned hurt, use it – don't cheat with it. Be as faithful to it as a scientist.'

At the typewriter, where Hemingway fought his biggest battles.

9

2 Childhood and Adolescence

Hemingway inherited a fascination with battle from his grandfathers, both of whom fought in the American Civil War (1860–65). His parents, Grace and Ed, were married in 1896 and set up home in Oak Park, a comfortable suburb of Chicago. Ed was an overworked and underpaid doctor. Grace had given up the possibility of an operatic career to marry him. During the first years of their marriage she provided the bulk of the family income by giving singing lessons. Oak Park, according to Hemingway was 'full of wide lawns and narrow minds'. He grew to despise the sober self-rightcousness

The Hemingway Family in 1906: Marcelline, Sunny, Dr Hemingway, Grace, Ursula and Ernest.

11

of Oak Park but there are few signs of rebellion during his childhood and adolescence. Ernest was born the second child of six, delivered by his father at home. He detested his Christian name and devised many nicknames to replace it: Wemmidge, Hemingstein and eventually Papa.

After he left home Hemingway almost always described his mother negatively. Grace dominated the household. She bullied her husband, humiliated him and eventually, Ernest felt, drove him to suicide. Nonetheless, Ernest gained from her the artistic sensitivity so important to his writing. He learnt his hunting and shooting skills from his father who was an expert woodsman. Ed Hemingway was a depressive man, subject to fits of temper and sporadic nervous collapses. Ernest developed a similarly uneven nature.

His childhood was peopled by women. He had four sisters and his only brother, Leicester, was born a full sixteen years after him. The female atmosphere of his home, combined with his father's lack of influence, must have made him feel that he needed to act in a consciously masculine fashion.

The house in Oak Park that Grace designed for her family. Young Ernest staged boxing matches in the conservatory.

Opposite
Hemingway's paternal grandfather, Anson; a staunch Republican.

13

Even as a young boy, Ernest was in combat, as his mother recorded: 'He delights in shooting imaginary wolves, bears, lions, buffalo, etc. Also likes to pretend he is a "soldser" . . . He is perfectly fearless after the first time bathing in the lake . . . When asked what he is afraid of, he shouts "fraid a nothing" with great gusto.' He was already building up his tough exterior, both afraid and denying his fear.

Ernest resented his mother's domineering self-centredness and his father's pliant passivity. When he was eighteen he sat watching his father working in the garden, holding a loaded gun and occasionally aiming at Ed's head in mock assassination. The imbalance of Grace and Ed's marriage became the subject of an early Hemingway story entitled 'The Doctor and the Doctor's Wife' (published in *In Our Time*). The doctor of the title is first humiliated by Indians who come to cut wood for him. An argument starts. The doctor threatens one of the Indians but is not man enough to carry out his threat. The doctor's second humiliation comes when the reader realizes how much he is controlled and cowed by his wife's every reaction:

> The doctor went out on the porch. The screen door slammed behind him. He heard his wife catch her breath when the door slammed.
> 'Sorry,' he said outside her window with the blinds drawn.
> 'It's alright, dear,' she said.

In another story, 'Fathers and Sons', Nick Adams (who may represent the young Hemingway) thinks about his father:

> '. . . his father was very nervous. Then, too, he was sentimental and, like most sentimental people, he was both cruel and abused. Also, he had much bad luck and it was not all of his own.'

Hemingway includes the mock assassinations that he performed on his father. Nick Adams sits by the woodshed and aims a loaded gun at his father: 'I can blow him to hell. I can kill him. Finally he felt his anger go out of him.'

Opposite *Ed and Grace Hemingway in 1897, a year after their marriage. Ernest had his father's eyes and some of his temperament.*

15

Hemingway at 17. After graduation he learnt to write as a reporter on the Kansas City Star.

16

When Ernest was not being tough he was reading, as every writer must, anything and everything. His nurse recalled: 'I'd find books stuffed under the mattress, in the pillowcase, everywhere. He read all the time – and books beyond his years.'

He worked hard at school and maintained a high grade average. He was once chosen to speak in church about schooling to a congregation of younger pupils. He participated in many sports, including boxing. Of his school-fellows, one found him 'exceedingly competitive towards everyone including his friends'; another thought he was 'egotistical, dogmatic and somewhat obnoxious'. In the school yearbook it was recorded that 'none are to be found more clever than Ernie'. In the two years before graduation he concentrated on writing. His stories were published in the school magazine *Tabula* and he was a journalist for the school newspaper.

His parents wanted him to go to college to study medicine, but in 1917 Hemingway left home to take a job with the *Kansas City Star* as a cub reporter. It was a good newspaper and the stylistic discipline imposed by his supervisor was valuable to Hemingway's development as a writer. He was told to use short sentences, avoid slang phrases and 'cultivate a plainness of expression all but devoid of adjectives'. He later remarked that 'those were the best rules I ever learnt for the business of writing'.

He told people that he tried to join the army to fight in the First World War, but that he was refused because of his poor eyesight. There is no record of this application which he probably invented to impress his fearlessness upon others. Another invention was his fantasy engagement to a Miss March, contrived in a letter to his mother, perhaps simply to irritate her, certainly to suggest that he was more mature than he was.

He joined the Red Cross in 1918. They sent him to Italy where, with the rank of lieutenant he bicycled along the front line handing out chocolates and cigarettes to soldiers. On the west bank of the Piave river, close to the Austrian border, a shell mortar exploded near him and he was injured by shrapnel in both legs.

As an injured American, he was automatically decorated by the Italian government. The wound was serious but the events around it provided Hemingway with the opportunity to embroider the truth. He told some that he had been hit by machine gun fire while shouldering a wounded man to safety. To others he made the more outrageous claim that he had fought with the Italian Arditi, a regiment of crack shock troops. He was proud of his wounds but perhaps less proud of the context in which he received them: better a shock trooper than a cycling chocolate vendor. He gained a sense of courage and invincibility from surviving his wounds. When Grace heard about the incident she wrote, 'It's great to be the mother of a hero.'

July 1918. Recovering in a Milan hospital, Hemingway smiles despite his wounds.

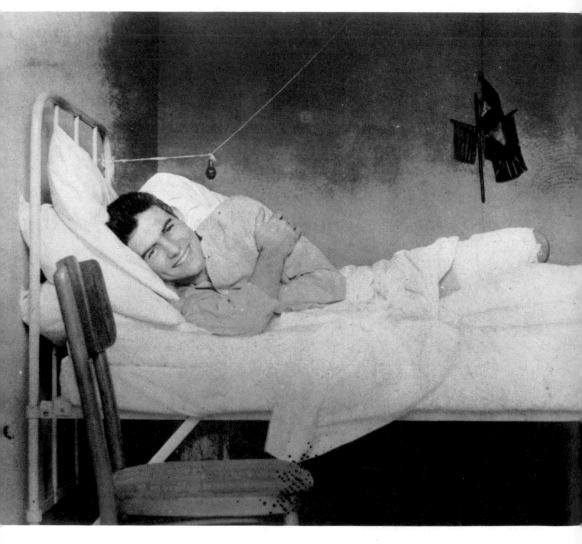

Italian troops march down a mountain road in 1918. Hemingway's wounding in Italy was to have a profound effect on him.

He was treated in Milan where he fell in love with his nurse, Agnes von Kurowsky. Their affair was platonic and when Hemingway returned to the USA he heard that he had lost Agnes to another man.

Many Hemingway commentators believe that his wounding in Italy was the key event in his early life. One claimed that 'nothing more important than that wounding was ever to happen to him.' He encouraged his public to believe that he had been permanently emotionally scarred by the First World War. He became the spokesman for a generation whose values and security

Opposite
*Back home in Oak Park, 1919.
Hemingway was proud of his uniform and his wounds.*

had been undermined by the horrors of the war. He came close to violent death and to love, two intertwined subjects that became central to his fiction. He was brave and he survived. His personal experience touched history for a few months. He felt that in this way he had won his manhood.

When he returned to the USA he was depressed by ordinary life. He felt deflated after the excitement of his affair with Agnes, his survival of the war and his sense of his own heroism. In the story 'Soldier's Home', Krebs, the main character, experiences 'a distaste for everything that happened to him in the war . . . because of the lies he had told.' In voicing Krebs's homecoming disillusion, Hemingway expressed some of his own. Like Krebs, he was in conflict with his parents. A letter from his father accuses Hemingway of having 'an iron heart of selfishness', while his mother scolded him: 'stop trading on your handsome face to fool little gullible girls, and neglecting your duty to God . . .'

Agnes von Kurowsky, who nursed Hemingway back to health and with whom he fell in love. She jilted him but won immortality as the inspiration behind Catherine in A Farewell to Arms.

20

In Chicago, he met Sherwood Anderson, an already established author who befriended and encouraged him. Hemingway had written some stories in Milan but had been unable to publish them on his return to the USA. Anderson read these stories, praised them and informed his young friend that the literary action was in Paris. He wrote letters of introduction to friends there in which he described Hemingway as a 'young fellow of extraordinary talent'.

In 1919, Hemingway secured a job on the *Toronto Star Weekly*. One of his acquaintances on the paper described him as follows: 'A more weird combination of quivering sensitivity and preoccupation with violence never

walked this earth.' In November 1920, he met Hadley Richardson, eight years his senior, who would become his first wife. Despite a series of unhappy affairs and a lifetime of family misery, Hadley was kind-hearted and submissive. Hemingway thought her red hair and high cheek bones beautiful. He gave her self-confidence and she rewarded him with unquestioning devotion. They were married in September 1921 in Horton Bay, Michigan. After a honeymoon in the Hemingway family summer house Ernest and Hadley sailed for Europe. 'The world's a jail,' Hadley said, 'and we're going to break it together.' Taking Anderson's advice, Hemingway was on his way to Paris.

Ernest marries Hadley Richardson on 3 September 1921. Left to Right: sisters Ursula and Carol, mother, brother Leicester and father.

3 Paris and the Literary Life

'If you are lucky enough to have lived in Paris as a young man,' Hemingway wrote, 'then wherever you go for the rest of your life, it stays with you, for Paris is a moveable feast.' The Hemingways rented a small apartment on the rue Cardinal Lemoine, in a working-class quarter of the city. Hemingway wrote in a rented room in another building or – when it was too cold – in one of the cafés. In his memoir, *A Moveable Feast* (1964), he stressed how poor he was in Paris. In fact, Hadley had a trust fund worth $3,000 a year and he could rely on $1,500 from his job as European correspondent of the *Toronto Star Weekly*. The Hemingways had enough money to live comfortably and by economizing on their flat and on clothes they were able to travel. Gertrude Stein, an American writer who lived in Paris, remarked that 'the Hemingways did what Ernest wanted', while Hadley tagged along. Post-war Paris offered Hemingway freedom from the stiff morality of mid-western USA. He embraced his newfound liberty with enthusiasm.

An acquaintance from this period recalled that 'Ernest was noble, a good friend, generous, passionate in his ideas and feelings, sentimental at times, extremely reflective and cautious; but above all, very, very complicated.' He was a complicated man working to achieve a simple style. His blue Paris notebooks are crammed with deletions and false starts. He tried 'to write one true sentence and go on from there,' striving for clarity,

Opposite *Rue Cardinal Lemoine in Paris, seen from a window of Hemingway's small rented apartment.*

24

Opposite *Ezra Pound. Hemingway taught him to box and Pound punched up Hemingway's prose in return.*

directness and economy of expression. Often it would take him an entire morning to perfect a single paragraph. He practised rigorous self-discipline, working alone from the early morning until lunchtime.

He was fortunate to be sharing Paris with some of the great literary innovators of the age. Ezra Pound, the American poet and trumpeter of other writers' talents, was an important teacher. He believed that prose should be free of all 'rhetorical din and luxurious [verbal] riot'.

> Pound was the man I liked and trusted most as a critic then, the man who believed in the *mot juste* – the one and only correct word to use – the man who taught me to distrust adjectives.

A second influence was Gertrude Stein. Hemingway spent many afternoons in Stein's flat, admiring her collection of paintings by Matisse, Picasso and Cézanne and talking about writing. 'Gert Stein and me are just like brothers,' Hemingway wrote. 'I learned wonderful rhythms in prose from her. She had . . . discovered many truths about rhythms and the uses of words in repetition.' Hemingway's friendship with Stein did not last, however. Hemingway fell out with her and they slighted one another in various ways for the rest of their lives.

Gertrude Stein, the modernist writer and collector, in Paris, 1925. She mothered Hemingway and helped to form his style.

Hemingway read avidly in Paris, learning from Turgenev, de Maupassant, Joseph Conrad, Tolstoy and many others. He borrowed books from Shakespeare and Company, a Paris bookshop, where he was introduced to James Joyce, an Irishman in self-imposed exile who had just completed his modernist novel *Ulysses*.

Outside Shakespeare and Company, the Paris left-bank bookshop. Sylvia Beach, the owner, looks admiringly at the ever-injured Hemingway, in 1928.

Hemingway admired Joyce's work and helped to smuggle copies of the banned text into the USA. Joyce's earlier work *Dubliners* was a collection of carefully interrelated short stories. The structure of this book probably influenced Hemingway when he came to arrange his own connected short stories for publication in *In Our Time*.

Hemingway had an extraordinary talent for making friends. Gerald Murphy, an American he met in Paris, recalled his 'enveloping personality, so physically huge and forceful. He overstated everything and talked so rapidly and so graphically that you found yourself agreeing with him.' He was by no means easy to get along with and another friend and helper, Robert McAlmon, described him as 'the hurt, sensitive boy, deliberately young and naïve, wanting to be brave and somehow on the defensive.' His flair for making friends was coupled with a tendency to fall out with them. He was jealous of other men's success and often abused and betrayed other writers, like Ford Madox Ford and John Dos Passos, who had been generous and welcoming to him. The force of his personality was such that despite his ingratitude and his mean streak he never lacked company: 'even his malice had a certain charm'. His obsession with courage drove him to prove himself by humiliating others. Donald Ogden Stewart, another American writer friend, remarked, 'he one by one knocked off the best friendships he ever had . . . I think it was a psychological fear he had that you might ask something of him.' Of all the friendships he made in Paris, only those with Pound and Joyce survived.

Not all of this time was spent in Paris. His reporting job obliged him to travel 10,000 miles by train in a single year. He wrote features rather than hard news and submitted pieces on the Genoa Conference, the Greco-Turkish War, the Lausanne Conference and the French-occupied Ruhr, all in a period of a few months. He interviewed Mussolini twice. In 1922, when the rest of the world was still admiring the man who would become the Fascist dictator of Italy, Hemingway described him as 'the biggest bluff in Europe'.

Hemingway believed that he could write well only from direct observation. 'It's very hard to get anything true on anything you haven't seen for yourself.' Journalism provided him with vital information and experience. Often he withheld the best stories from his reports and used them in his fiction. Some found this practice cynical, but for Hemingway fiction would always be more important than journalism.

The Hemingways found the time and money to ski in Italy and Switzerland, and to tour the Black Forest, northern Italy and Spain. In December 1922, before one of these skiing trips, Hadley decided to pack all her husband's manuscripts and the carbon copies in one suitcase which was stolen from her train compartment. Hemingway lost the greater bulk of the writing he had done in a year. He felt 'so badly about the loss that [he] would almost have resorted to surgery in order to forget it.' Hadley believed that he 'never recovered from the pain of this irreparable loss.' In *A Moveable Feast*, Hemingway claimed that 'it was probably good for me to lose my early work'. Yet, at the time, he felt he would never write again. Two stories survived because they were in the post to magazines, and one of these, 'My Old Man', was published in the *Best Stories of 1923*.

In the winter of 1922–3, Hadley became pregnant. Imminent fatherhood only served to deepen the resentment that Hemingway already felt about the lost manuscripts. Gertrude Stein recalled that Hemingway 'announced that his wife was enceinte [pregnant] and then with great bitterness, and I, I am too young to be a father.' In the summer, the Hemingways visited northern Spain. At the festival of San Fermin in Pamplona, Hemingway fell in love with bullfighting. He described the sport as 'just like having a ringside seat

at the war with nothing going to happen to you.' It answered his fascination with violent death and the testing of human courage. He admired the skill and nerve of bullfighters, their 'grace under pressure', and identified himself with them. During the drunken excitement of the festival Hemingway was misreported as being gored by a bull while saving a friend from danger. On this and many other occasions, he allowed the newspapers to invent a public image for him. By 1928, he had the unearned reputation of being a 'semi-professional prizefighter . . . an expert in skiing . . . an amateur toreador' and a war hero. Kenneth Lynn, one of his biographers, is right to point out that Hemingway 'would feel impelled to live up to his public image' and that 'from the early thirties onward, the pitiless glare of the spotlight . . . would interfere with the free working of his creative imagination.'

Opposite *Daring young men run in front of the bulls to display their courage at Pamplona, Spain, the location for* Fiesta.

In August 1923 the Hemingways sailed for Toronto where their son, John Nicanor, was to be born. In the same month, *Three Stories and Ten Poems*, Hemingway's first book, was privately printed by McAlmon in an edition of 300 copies. In March 1924, the Three Mountains Press published *in our time*, a 38-page booklet containing eighteen vignettes, in a tiny edition of 170. These non-commercial publications contained powerful evidence of Hemingway's development. The influential critic, Edmund Wilson, referred to Hemingway's work as 'prose of the first distinction' and likened it to the fiction of Sherwood Anderson. *In our time* consists of brief observations of violent incidents recounted in a terse, stripped style. Injury, danger and death, in war and in the bullring, are described in a hard-boiled tone. Pound had noticed a 'self-hardening process' in Hemingway: *in our time* inaugurates the cult of toughness that characterized much of Hemingway's subsequent work. The sketches seem fragmentary but, 'when read together they all hook up', as Hemingway wrote to Pound. While the author enjoyed the praise of his contemporaries, his parents returned their six copies of the book to the publisher, disgusted by their son's work.

When he returned to Paris, Hemingway wrote nine new stories. He interleaved these with the sketches from *in our time* to form a manuscript long enough for commercial publication. He called this bigger collection

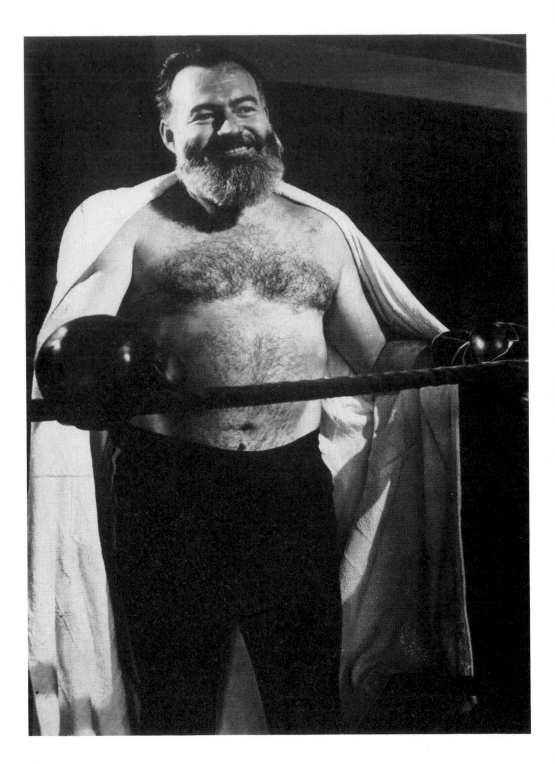

In Our Time and had it accepted by the New York house, Boni and Liverwright, in 1925. The $200 advance was much needed, for Hemingway had resigned from his job with the *Toronto Star* and Hadley's trust fund had been whittled away by poor investments. His stories were being published in small literary journals like Ford's *Transatlantic Review*, but the high-paying American magazines still rejected his work.

With the publication of *In Our Time* Hemingway's literary reputation was firmly established, but his personal life began to crumble. His son, known as Mr Bumby, cried persistently and more noise came from the sawmill above which the Hemingways now lived. Fatherhood and financial insecurity made him increasingly dissatisfied with his marriage. He developed a passion for Lady Duff Twysden, an English 'alcoholic nymphomaniac' who became the model for Brett Ashley, the heroine of *The Sun Also Rises* (published in Britain as *Fiesta*). During a disastrous trip to Pamplona in the summer of 1925, Hemingway flirted with Duff while Harold Loeb, a wealthy Jewish American, had an affair with her. Hemingway and Loeb came close to a fistfight. Soon after the crush on Duff had subsided, Hemingway fell in love with the slim, glamorously-attired Pauline Pfeiffer. Hadley, busy with her baby and dowdy in old clothes, passively accepted her humiliation. His moralizing mother, hearing rumours about Hemingway's marital problems, asked him in a letter if he had 'ceased to be interested in loyalty, nobility, honour and fineness of life.'

Hemingway began his affair with Pauline in February 1926 and left Hadley in August. His love letters to Pauline were tainted by guilt about his infidelity to Hadley. He was both appalled and thrilled by the destructiveness of his actions. He contemplated suicide. When he returned to the flat above the sawmill to collect his possessions he broke down and cried. At the time, when friends asked him why he was separating from Hadley he said, 'because I am a son of a bitch'. In *A Moveable Feast*, he looked back with sentimental longing and suggested that 'the rich' had seduced him away from a happy marriage. This marked the beginning of a lifelong habit of blaming others for his own weaknesses, his own choices. By marrying Pauline in May 1927, Hemingway

Opposite By 1928 Hemingway had the unearned reputation of being a 'semi-professional prizefighter': an image he allowed the press to invent for him.

freed himself of financial anxieties, but he would always remain trapped by his guilt about Hadley. In 1942 he was still writing loving letters to her. 'I wish I had died

July 1926. During the Festival of San Fermin at Pamplona, Hemingway sits between Pauline and Hadley.

before I loved anyone but her,' he wrote in *A Moveable Feast*. In Paris, where he learnt his craft, he lost some of his integrity.

4 Early Stories and a First Novel

With the publication of *In Our Time* in the USA, Hemingway was recognized as a major talent by already established contemporaries. D.H. Lawrence wrote that, 'It is a short book: and it does not pretend to be about one man. But it is . . . the sketches are short, sharp, vivid and most of them excellent.' Edmund Wilson found Hemingway 'remarkably successful in suggesting moral values by a series of simple statements.'

Eight of the fifteen stories in *In Our Time* are about Nick Adams. Six out of these eight draw on Hemingway's early experiences in Michigan where his family had a summer house. It is generally accepted that Nick Adams is Hemingway in these stories. The collection opens and closes with Michigan stories and between these are sandwiched tales set in Europe where we are given glimpses of the war in Italy and of Americans abroad.

Hemingway was working to perfect a method by which feelings could be communicated through the details of a story without being baldly stated. He compared his technique to an iceberg:

> I always try to write on the principle of the iceberg. There is seven-eights of it underwater for every part that shows. Anything you know you can eliminate and it only strengthens your iceberg. It is the part that doesn't show.

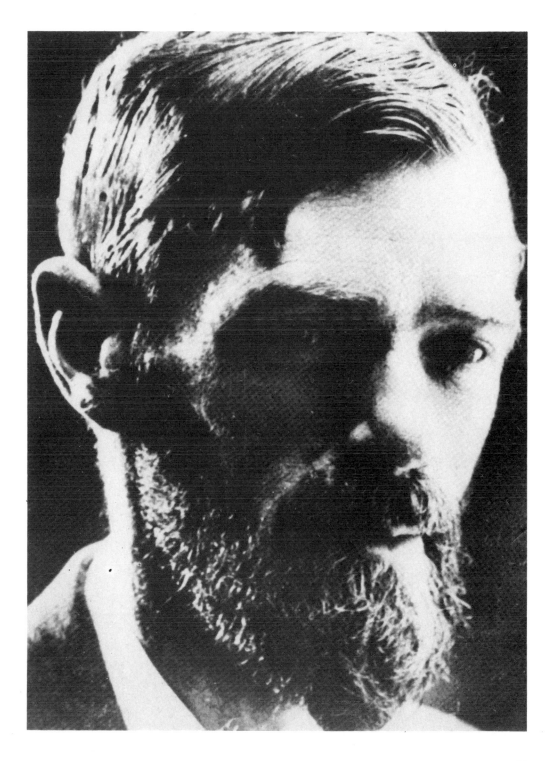

In 'Soldier's Home', a story about a man returning from war and trying to re-adapt to American life, Hemingway applies the 'iceberg principle' so that the soldier's disillusionment and disorientation are submerged in the details of the narrative. The climax of the story comes when the soldier lies to his mother, telling her he loves her when he does not. At this point Hemingway tells us what is already apparent: 'Still, none of it had touched him. He had felt sorry for his mother and she had made him lie.' If Hemingway revealed too much of the iceberg in 'Soldier's Home', he showed too little of it in 'Out of Season'. This story, set in Italy, is about an old man who guides a young American couple to a trout river and encourages them to fish out of season. The key event in the story, the suicide of the old man, is left out altogether. Clearly, too much is omitted in 'Out of Season': there are no hints in the tale to help the reader guess the ending.

These two stories suggest that Hemingway was experimenting with the principle of omission in *In Our Time*. In the two-part story that ends the collection, 'The Big Two-Hearted River', he succeeds in refining this technique. Nick Adams sets out on a fishing trip. He takes a train to a town which has been burnt to the ground – 'the country was burnt over and changed but that did not matter'. He walks into the countryside: 'He felt he had everything behind him, the need for thinking, the need to write, other things. It was all back of him.' Nick walks all day and makes camp. The inside of his tent feels like home. Just what he has left behind remains obscure, but the threat of his past is always present in the atmosphere of the story. 'His mind was starting to work. He knew he could choke it because he was tired enough'. The word 'choke' suggests the forcible restraint of thought. Violent images disturb the peace and solitude of the camp Nick has made deep in the woods. At the end of part one he kills a mosquito, incinerating it with a match.

Between parts one and two, Hemingway inserted a paragraph which describes a man being hanged at dawn in an American County jail. The condemned man's terror and the hollow words of the priest – 'Be a man, my son' – add to the sense of something brutal or shocking underlying the fishing trip. In part two, we rejoin Nick in the

Fishing was the apparent subject of two great early stories, 'Out of Season' and 'The Big Two-hearted River'.

morning. The calm with which he methodically cooks breakfast, catches bait and notes details of the countryside seems sinister after the panic of the hanging. He fishes the trout stream and contemplates fishing a swamp where he knows the biggest trout will be:

> In the fast water, in the deep light, the fishing would be tragic. In the swamp fishing was a tragic adventure. Nick did not want it.

The word 'tragic' is strong in this context and hints at other tragedies which Nick does not want to remember.

The powerful atmosphere of 'Big Two-Hearted River' is created out of the tightly controlled descriptions of the countryside and the character's actions. Many details hint at Nick's state of mind, which is evoked without being explained. 'Big Two-Hearted River' demonstrates

43

Hemingway's mastery of the 'iceberg' method. The atmosphere of unease is intense, although the source of that unease is almost completely hidden. Years later, in *A Moveable Feast* he stated that 'the story was about coming back from the war but there was no mention of the war in it.'

Between the publication of *In Our Time* and his first novel, *Fiesta* Hemingway wrote a parody called *The Torrents of Spring*. In this short book he viciously attacked the work of Sherwood Anderson and Gertrude Stein. *The Torrents of Spring* is certainly funny but mostly at the expense of two writers who had helped and influenced Hemingway. In satirizing those who had helped form his style Hemingway was able to deny their influence. The book was published by Scribners, where Hemingway, Scott Fitzgerald and Thomas Wolfe were all edited by Max Perkins. Perkins had helped to nurture Fitzgerald's talent. In return, Fitzgerald had alerted Perkins to the quality of Hemingway's work.

Hemingway and Fitzgerald met in Paris just after the publication of Fitzgerald's *The Great Gatsby* in 1925. Their friendship was hampered by Scott's alcoholism and Ernest's jealousy. Fitzgerald's influence on Hemingway is underrated. Later, Hemingway did what he could to disparage Fitzgerald's character and so deny the influence. Despite the critical acclaim that Fitzgerald was receiving at the time he was convinced that the younger Hemingway was the greater writer. Another novelist, Glenway Wescott, noted that Fitzgerald 'not only said but, I believe, honestly felt that Hemingway was inimitably, essentially superior . . . Hemingway could be entrusted with the graver responsibilities and higher rewards, such as glory, immortality.' Hemingway found Fitzgerald 'a little embarassing from his tendency always to hero-worship.'

Scott's wife, Zelda, was neurotic, hard-drinking and envied her husband's literary success. He struggled under the weight of his own and Zelda's extravagances and had to write stories for magazines to cover his bills. He deliberately doctored these stories so that they conformed to the house style of the commissioning magazine. This commercial habit met with Hemingway's contempt. It is ironic that in later life the Hemingway who chastised Fitzgerald for his drinking and magazine

work should be destroyed by alcohol and write second-rate work for high-paying magazines. In *A Moveable Feast*, written when Fitzgerald's reputation was posthumously soaring, Hemingway wrote with cruel, apparent candour about the behaviour of the young Scott. Every anecdote is slanted to emphasize Fitzgerald's silliness and self-pity, so that he seems a hypochondriac, weak-headed wastrel.

If Hemingway found the man ridiculous, he felt the opposite about the work. He considered *The Great Gatsby* 'an absolutely first-rate book'. Hemingway's debunking of Fitzgerald's personality was probably spurred by envy: *Gatsby* achieved immediate critical success. More importantly, it was after reading *Gatsby* that Hemingway set to work on *Fiesta* (published in the USA as *The Sun Also Rises*), his first and possibly best novel. Hemingway took up the challenge of *Gatsby* and tried to surpass it.

Fiesta is set in Paris and Pamplona (northern Spain). It tells the story of a group of expatriate English and Americans, hard-drinking people who have lost touch with moral values. In its treatment of humanity *Fiesta* is disillusioned and sometimes very funny. Hemingway insisted that the true hero of the book was the earth itself, 'which abideth forever' while people are born and die. This preference for the land over its people, already evident in 'The Big Two-Hearted River', was to be stressed in *The Green Hills of Africa*: 'I had loved the country all my life; the country was always better than the people'. The only beauty that remains untainted in *Fiesta* is that of place. The people are flawed by lust, jealousy, dishonesty and carelessness. The book was not a 'hollow, bitter satire,' Hemingway wrote, 'but a damned tragedy with the earth abiding forever as the hero.'

Fiesta is narrated by Jake Barnes, an American reporter living in Paris. He is in love with Brett Ashley, an English aristocrat, alcoholic and promiscuous. Her style and her passion dominate the novel, precipitating its key events and its climax. Jake suffers from a war wound: although he feels sexual desire for Brett he cannot achieve relief from that desire. This disability is one of the main sources of tension in the book and symbolizes the moral impotence of the characters.

Opposite *July, 1925. To Hemingway's left are Duff Twysden, the model for Brett Ashley in* Fiesta, *and Hadley, a wife fast losing her grip on her husband.*

Robert Cohn, the book's anti-hero, is a Jewish American, a Princeton graduate and a boxer. He believes that a brief fling with Brett gives him a claim to her heart. These characters, along with Jake's witty friend Bill and the bankrupt Mike Campbell whom Brett is supposed to be marrying, join up to go to the festival of San Fermin in Pamplona.

Before the festival starts, Jake and Bill take a bus up into the Pyrenees to Burgete to fish for trout in the Irati river. The period in Burgete is the paradise of *Fiesta*. The beauty and heroism of the earth dominate; irony has no bitterness and the absence of Brett and Cohn dispels jealousy and frustration.

> Beyond the fields we crossed another fast-flowing stream. A sandy road led down to the ford and beyond into the woods. The path crossed the stream on another foot-log below the ford, and joined the road, and we went into the woods.
>
> It was a beech wood and the trees were very old. Their roots bulked above the ground and the branches were twisted. We walked on the road between the thick trunks of the old beeches and the sunlight came through the leaves in light patches on the grass. The trees were big, and the foliage was thick but it was not gloomy. There was no undergrowth, only the smooth grass, very green and fresh, and the big grey trees well spaced as though it were a park.
>
> 'This is country,' Bill said.

Bill and Jake take pleasure in each other's company. Hemingway uses their light banter as a camouflage behind which to slip in some thematic points, as when Bill teases Jake:

> 'You're an expatriate. You've lost touch with the soil. You get precious. Fake European standards have ruined you. You drink yourself to death. You become obsessed with sex . . .'

Bill then makes an unfortunate reference to sexual impotence. Neither Jake nor the reader are allowed to forget Jake's sexual disability for long.

The main characters meet in Pamplona for the Fiesta. They watch the running of the bulls through the streets of the old town. Brett is fascinated by the brute beauty of the beasts. When the first bullfight takes place the

sexual passion aroused by Brett is contrasted to *aficion*, the Spanish 'passion' for bullfighting. Pedro Romero, the youngest and most graceful of the *torreros* has *aficion*; Jake, unusually for an American, has it as a spectator. *Aficion*, a passion for the tragic ritual in which the bull must always die and the man risks his life, is a passion for destruction. Similarly Brett's sexual passion causes destruction. The passion she arouses in Cohn makes him fauning, absurd and then dangerous.

Torla, a village in the Pyrenees. The sort of village that Bill and Jake fished near in Fiesta.

Brett's passion for Pedro Romero is a corrupting threat to the young fighter. She feels she has no control over her desire. '"I don't say it's right. It's right for me though. God knows, I've never felt such a bitch."' The formal physical destruction of the bullfight acts as a parallel to the more subtle emotional and spiritual destructiveness of the characters.

Hemingway depicts *aficion* as pure, and sexual passion as sullied, dirty, corrupt. When Jake helps to bring about the affair between Brett and Romero he is the pimp who pollutes the young man's purity, endangering something he admires and loves – Romero's genius in the bullring – for the sake of Brett, whom he loves and cannot have.

A Spanish bullfight. In this scene the Picador weakens the bull by placing a pic in the shoulder muscle.

Hemingway often compared bullfighting to writing and the 'holding of his purity of line through the maximum of exposure' became one of his aesthetic ideals: to describe the emotion behind a situation with unflinching honesty and never to be swayed from his clear, simple style in so doing. Through most of *Fiesta* Hemingway stays close to this ideal and only falls short of it when he allows Jake's self-pity and sentimentality to introduce a false tone into the prose.

The climax comes when Cohn, in a jealous rage, punches Jake, Mike and Romero. Romero alone remains undefeated. However many times Cohn knocks him down, he gets up again and tries to hit Cohn; finally, Cohn refuses to hit Romero any more and Romero promises to kill him. Cohn disappears, from Pamplona and from the novel, stripped of all dignity, shut out from our pity. In the bullring the next day, Romero, his face bruised, his body aching, kills with classic grace, slaughtering his last bull right below Brett.

After a brief affair, Brett leaves Romero, having decided to ruin him no further. She and Jake ride through Madrid in a carriage. The atmosphere of tragic impossibility is tinged by Jake's irony right to the last:

> 'Oh, Jake,' Brett said, 'we could have had such a damned good time together.'
> 'Yes,' I said. 'Isn't it pretty to think so.'

Hemingway conveys the full emotion of Brett and Jake's unfulfillable love. Despite her being a self-confessed 'bitch', despite his self-pity, we experience a searing feeling of loss. Hemingway's ability to create a sense of place – in Paris, Pamplona and Burgete – fleshes out his exploration of the relationship between passion and destruction, love and death. The dialogue is terse, accurate and carries much of the burden of characterization. In 1933, Hemingway summarized the things he thought a good book should have:

> All good books are alike in that they are truer than if they really happened and after you are finished reading one you feel that all that happened to you and afterwards it all belongs to you; the good and the bad, the ecstasy, the remorse and the sorrow, the people and the places and how the weather was.

Opposite *Paris, Rue de la Paix*. Fiesta *opens with a sketch of expatriate life in Paris. Hemingway's memoir,* A Moveable Feast, *pays homage to Paris.*

By these standards, *Fiesta* is a success. Hemingway wrote the book in two hectic months during the summer of 1925. 'Towards the end it was like a fever,' he wrote. He spent the next six months carefully revising and cutting the text. 'The most essential gift for a good writer,' Hemingway wrote, 'is a built-in, shock-proof, shit-detector. This is the writer's radar.' He believed that a book could often be judged by what the author eliminated. He excised many blunt statements of feeling and refined his dialogue and imagery so that these carried his emotional message. Scribners published it in October 1926.

The book's original American title, *The Sun Also Rises* is culled from a passage in Ecclesiastes: 'One generation passeth away and another generation cometh; but the earth abideth forever . . . The sun also ariseth . . .' This quotation and another gleaned from conversation with Gertrude Stein – 'You are all a lost generation' – were used on the title page of the first edition. Hemingway's notebooks reveal that he considered using 'The Lost Generation' as his title at one stage. It was a catchy phrase and summed up the experience of people who had 'grown up to find all Gods dead, all wars fought, all faith in man shaken' (as Fitzgerald put it in his first novel, *This Side of Paradise*, 1921).

Fiesta was well reviewed, and the behaviour of Brett and the other characters had a strong effect on Hemingway's readers. Journalists noted that college girls were 'modelling themselves on Lady Brett'. Edmund Wilson wrote in 1927 that Hemingway:

> expressed the romantic disillusion and set the favourite pose of the period. It was the moment of gallantry in heartbreak, grim nonchalant banter and heroic dissipation. The great watchword was 'Have a drink' and in the bars of New York and Paris the people were getting to talk like Hemingway.

Hemingway's mother Grace, never a frequenter of bars, thought that *Fiesta* was 'One of the filthiest books of the year'.

Fitzgerald's *The Great Gatsby* was published in April 1925, a few months before Hemingway commenced writing *Fiesta*. Hemingway had read *Gatsby* and the reviews of it. There are remarkable similarities between the two books. Hemingway went so far as to satirize

Gatsby in the Burgete episode of *Fiesta* where Jake and Bill make jesting references to 'irony and pity', two of the qualities that one reviewer had identified in *Gatsby*.

Gatsby is a tale of the destructiveness of passion. Its mood is that of 'romantic disillusion' and it concludes

Robert Redford as Jay Gatsby in the film version of The Great Gatsby.

with a eulogy to the 'breast of the new green world' (i.e. the American soil): although the characters are either dead or ruined by the end, the earth – as in *Fiesta* – remains. Fitzgerald's theme was the 'vast carelessness of the rich', a carelessness which Brett, Cohn and Jake exhibit in their treatment of each other and Romero. Both books take the loss of love and love's destruction as their subject and are played out in an atmosphere of aimless revelry and drunken bitterness. Nick Carraway, the narrator of *The Great Gatsby*, is a sentimentalist who acts as a pimp between the hero and the heroine, as Jake does between Brett and Romero. The narrators of both novels try to remain detached from the corruption they observe, but are finally drawn in and stained by it. Perhaps, in view of the two books' similarities, it is not surprising that Hemingway did everything he could, in *A Moveable Feast*, to depict Fitzgerald as a hopeless drunk and an emotional failure. He also suppressed the fact that Fitzgerald helped him edit the first two chapters of *Fiesta*. Like Gertrude Stein and Sherwood Anderson before him, Fitzgerald was another important influence on Hemingway's development; like them, he was thanked with slander and betrayal.

In 1927, while Hemingway and Pauline took a holiday in Spain, revisiting some of the locations of *Fiesta*, Hemingway's next book, *Men Without Women*, was published in the USA. In three months 15,000 copies were sold, an enormous figure for a collection of short stories. The book's title describes the predominantly masculine world of its stories: bullfighters, gangsters, soldiers and boxers were Hemingway's characters. Yet some of the best stories are about the difficulties of relationships between men and women, the conflict between their different needs and aspirations. In one of the best stories of the collection, 'Hills Like White Elephants', a man tries to manipulate his lover into having an abortion; the hopeless alienation which their situation and his attitude create is delicately communicated through charged dialogue.

If Hemingway was angry with his mother for her reaction to *Fiesta*, he sought revenge in the final story of *Men Without Women*. In 'Now I Lay Me', he took many details from his parents' lives and used them to portray a wife who destroys her husband.

5 The Public Hero in Private Decline

Hemingway left Europe for the USA in 1928. He and Pauline moved to Key West on the southern tip of Florida. Hemingway's second son, Patrick, was born in Kansas City in June. He had wanted a daughter and was disappointed by the arrival of a second son. By way of compensation, he developed the habit of calling his close women friends 'daughter', and many of his friends now referred to him as 'Papa', even though he was not yet thirty.

Opposite
Hemingway with his new wife, Pauline, on the beach at San Sebastian, two months after their wedding, July 1927.

Key West in Florida, Hemingway's base during the 1930s.

While Pauline was giving birth to a son, Hemingway was conceiving and hatching *A Farewell to Arms*. As he came close to completing the novel he learned that his father had committed suicide, shooting himself with the pistol his grandfather had used during the Civil War. Hemingway's initial, shocked response was 'I'll probably go the same way myself'. He was doubly devastated, both by the fact of his father's death and the manner of it. He became obsessed with his father's cowardice. In 1948 he wrote to a friend: 'My mother is an all-time, all-American bitch and she would make a pack-mule shoot herself; let alone poor bloody father.'

Hemingway staunched his grief while finishing *A Farewell to Arms*. As he tried to control his own emotions he supressed many of his characters' feelings. The book was completed in January 1929 and then published in September.

Farewell continues Hemingway's exploration of the twinned themes of love and death and is set against the backcloth of the First World War in Italy. The hero, Frederick Henry, is an American ambulance driver working with the Italians on the Austrian front. Like his creator, Frederick Henry is wounded and falls in love with the nurse who cares for him. Agnes Von Kurowsky is transformed into a statuesque Englishwoman called Catherine Barkley. Her fiancé has died in the trenches and his death contributes to the atmosphere of imminent tragedy that overhangs the love affair between Catherine and Frederick. When she becomes pregnant the lovers flee to Switzerland where Catherine dies in childbirth. Hemingway's second novel describes 'the tragedy he felt was inherent in sexual love'. The lovers pay for their happiness with a pregnancy that leads to death. That this should happen after they have apparently escaped the danger of war, makes Catherine's death more painful, more ironic.

Although Catherine is a less fully-realized character than Brett in *Fiesta*, her death is heartbreaking. Death and defeat conquer love and courage, but only after Hemingway has made us experience the richness of love and the struggle for bravery through our sympathy with his characters. As with Desdemona in *Othello*, Catherine's death seems unbearable and pointless, but it is more than that, for it highlights her beauty and her

In the late summer of that year
we lived in a house in a village that

~~In the night we heard the troops~~

looked across the river and the plain to the
mountains. The water in the river clear
boulders and The river bed was white pebbles, and dry white
the water was clear and swiftly moving and blue in the
bed of white pebbles and white boulders and
~~there were always~~ troops went by the house
and down the ~~roads~~ road and the dust
they raised powdered the leaves of the trees,
the trunks of the trees too were dusty and the
leaves fell early that year and we saw
~~saw~~ the troops marching along the road and
the dust rising and leaves stirred by the breeze
the soldiers marching and afterwards the
road bare and white except for the leaves,

61

capacity to love while alive. In the following passage Frederick Henry struggles with the news that Catherine is dying:

'Mrs. Henry has had a haemorrhage.'
'Can I go in?'
'No, not yet. The doctor is with her.'
'Is it dangerous?'
'It is very dangerous.' The nurse went into the room and shut the door. I sat outside in the hall. Everything was gone inside of me. I did not think. I could not think. I knew she was going to die and I prayed that she would not. Don't let her die. Oh, God, please don't let her die. I'll do anything for you if you won't let her die. Please, please, please, dear God, don't let her die. Dear God, don't let her die.

Dorothy Parker in 1939. A fellow writer who worshipped Hemingway and helped build up the Hemingway myth.

A Farewell to Arms was one of Hemingway's most successful books. It sold a million and a half copies by the time of his death in 1961. With its publication his reputation peaked. The book was supremely well-reviewed. The American writer Dorothy Parker wrote a profile of Hemingway in the *New Yorker* magazine in 1929, which further inflated his image as public hero. She wrote that he 'has the most profound bravery that it has ever been my privilege to see.' Hemingway played on this legend, allowing people to believe that 'his life, his writing, his public personality and his private thoughts were all of a piece'. One friend noted:

> No one was more conscious than Ernest of the figure and image he possessed in the minds of the American press and reading public . . . He deliberately set out to keep the legend and image alive in the form he wanted it.

Pauline's Uncle Gus bought her a house in Key West in 1931. Unearned luxuries continued to come Hemingway's way – Gus gave him $25,000 for an African safari in 1933. Hemingway developed a taste for the company of the very rich; in Florida, cut off from literary friendship, he went deep sea fishing with wealthy companions. During this period he wrote *Death in the Afternoon*, an overlong, sometimes self-indulgent history of bullfighting which included asides on Spanish culture and personal reminiscence. Too conscious of the shadow of his own legend, Hemingway adopted an overbearing tone and an artificial style. He indulged his fascination with death and killing. Although the book has its moments it was, all in all, a failure.

The Key West house bought for the Hemingways by Pauline's Uncle Gus.

Hemingway's next collection of short stories, *Winner Take Nothing* (1933), received poor reviews but sold well. His literary reputation was taking a downward turn and his pride was assaulted by Gertrude Stein's vengeful jibes (in *The Autobiography of Alice B. Toklas*) that he was 'yellow' and 'looks like a modern and smells of the museums'.

Pauline gave birth to another son in 1931. In the same year Hemingway started an affair with the manic depressive Jane Mason. She was more beautiful than any of his wives, a sportswoman, a big drinker. In 1933, she attempted suicide, by jumping out of a window and

Jane Mason, Hemingway's mistress during the early 1930s, at home in Havana with her husband and children.

breaking her back. Hemingway referred to her with black humour as 'the girl who fell for me literally'.

During the African safari of 1933–4 Hemingway wrote *The Green Hills of Africa* (1935). Hemingway's non-fiction African book was, in the opinion of Edmund Wilson, 'one of the only books ever written which make Africa and its animals seem dull. Almost the only thing we learn about the animals is that Hemingway wants to kill them.' The artistic failure of *Green Hills* was balanced by the brilliance of two short stories, 'The Snows of Kilimanjaro' and 'The Short Happy Life of Francis Macomber', both set on the African plains.

'Macomber' is about victory over fear during a big-

Hunter and prey in East Africa, January 1934. This safari inspired a weak book (The Green Hills of Africa) *and two very strong short stories.*

game shoot. The wealthy Macomber and his wife Margot (modelled on Jane Mason) 'had a sound basis of union. Margot was too beautiful for Macomber to divorce her and Macomber had too much money for Margot ever to leave him.' Wilson, their paid guide and white hunter, is a fearless, red-faced Englishman. The story documents the shift in power between these three characters. Macomber gives in to his terror – while stalking a wounded lion he turns and runs. Margot chides her husband's cowardice. Wilson ponders her behaviour: 'How should a woman act when she discovers her husband is a bloody coward? She's damn cruel, but they're all cruel.' Margot is seduced by Wilson's contrasting

bravery and sleeps with him. Macomber hunts buffalo and finds that, 'for the first time in his life he really felt wholly without fear.' His newfound courage terrifies Margot; his fear, through which she could control him, is gone. Wilson admires his client's transformation: 'Fear gone like an operation. Something else grew in its place. Main thing a man had. Made him into a man. Women knew it too.' Macomber stalks a wounded buffalo and stands his ground when the beast charges him. Margot shoots – at the buffalo? at her husband? – the bullet kills Macomber: she has destroyed the man she can no longer dominate.

'The Snows of Kilimanjaro' describes the last twenty-four hours of a writer's life as he dies of gangrene in an African camp. His rich wife nurses him. They quarrel. He reflects on his life, all the things he has left unwritten, his failures. Some of the dying writer's thoughts are eerily prophetic of Hemingway's future:

> He had destroyed his talent himself . . . by not using it, by betrayals of himself and what he believed in, by drinking so much that he blunted the edge of his perception, by laziness, by sloth . . .

The story is an imaginative *tour de force* in which Hemingway faces death and failure, creating an appalling reality out of the destruction of love and talent. There is nothing sentimental or false in the tone of the piece. Death approaches, the vultures wheel and gather, the expected plane never arrives.

The successes of 'Macomber' and 'Kilimanjaro' (coupled with the failures of *Death in the Afternoon* and *Green Hills of Africa*) illustrate an important point: Hemingway always wrote better when he absorbed his own experience into the structure of fiction than when he wrote as a reporter or a historian. After a period of poor work, he transformed his preoccupation with death, slow or violent, and his growing doubts about his wealthy wife, into two of his best short stories. His vision of life was darkening. When the affair with Jane Mason ended in 1936 he was deeply depressed and wrote to a friend: 'thought I was facing impotence, inability to write, insomnia and was going to blow my lousy head off.'

6 Another War, Another Wife

Hemingway met Martha Gellhorn in 1936. She was a writer and journalist, well-connected and independent in contrast to Hemingway's first two wives who were both of submissive, passive temperaments. Her literary talent had been compared to her future husband's before they met. 'Hemingway does not write more authentic American speech. Nor can he teach Martha Gellhorn anything about economy of language.' In 1940 she became his third wife.

1936 was also the year in which the Civil War broke out in Spain. The elected left-wing government, known as the Loyalists, were fighting the Fascists, led by General Francisco Franco and supported by Hitler and Mussolini. The Loyalists enjoyed the backing of Stalin's USSR and the International Brigades. Hemingway loved Spain and remained fascinated by war. He was glad to leave Key West: 'Nothing's really happening to me here and I've got to get out . . . In Spain maybe it's the big parade starting again.' He believed that 'Civil war is the best war for a writer, the most complete.' During the Spanish Civil War he gathered material for one of his best, most complete novels, *For Whom the Bell Tolls*.

Until the mid 1930s, Hemingway's work had shown little sign of political commitment. In 1937, he published *To Have and Have Not*, the only novel he located in the USA. Curiously, he fails to bring Key West, Florida, to life and his hero, Harry Morgan, fisherman-turned-

Opposite Gary Cooper (who starred in the films of A Farewell to Arms *and* For Whom the Bell Tolls*), Martha Gellhorn (Hemingway's third wife), Mrs Gary Cooper and an unshaven Hemingway in the 1930s.*

Hemingway with other reporters during the Spanish Civil War, 1937.

smuggler, is neither sympathetic nor believable. Left-wing critics, however, praised the book in spite of its obvious weaknesses because it showed signs of a new awareness of social injustices and inequalities.

During the Spanish conflict Hemingway certainly sided with the have-nots, the peasants, and the down-trodden workers. He helped to make a film, *The Spanish Earth*, which was used to raise funds for the Loyalist cause. In the articles he wrote from Spain as a correspondent for the North American Newspaper Alliance his allegiance was clearly with the Loyalists. Martha noted sardonically that 'I think it was the only time in his life when he was not the most important thing there was.' He may have 'lacked political sophistication' (as one of his biographers complains) in blindly embracing the Loyalist cause. The glaring wrongness of Fascism led him and many other intellectuals, including George Orwell, to disregard the more carefully concealed evils of the Communist element in the Loyalist left.

Hemingway was accompanied by Martha on his visits to Spain. They reported on battles together. He praised her coolness under fire and, as usual, exaggerated his own bravery. However, he did show considerable courage and know-how on one occasion, saving himself and other reporters during a dangerous river crossing. His affair with Martha became public knowledge in Madrid during an air raid when they were seen emerging from the same bedroom. He wrote a play, *The Fifth Column*, about the Fascist seige of Madrid but his work was overshadowed by the novel he started writing about the war in 1939.

Captured Communists near Madrid, November 1936.

Rebel (left-wing) troops move towards Madrid, 1938. The Spanish Civil War is the setting for Hemingway's powerful novel, For Whom the Bell Tolls.

For Whom the Bell Tolls is set in the Sierra mountain range of Segovia and spans the last three days of its hero's life. Robert Jordan, an American teacher and dynamite expert, blows up bridges for the Loyalists. At the beginning of the novel he joins up with a band of Loyalist guerillas and falls in love with one of the women, Maria. Hemingway balances the story of the love affair between Jordan and Maria with a detailed picture of life behind enemy lines during wartime. The action is seen from Jordan's point of view. Through his flashbacks we learn about the wider arena of the war, in Madrid and elsewhere. Pilar, the wife of the guerilla leader, describes her part in the slaughter of Fascists at Ronda. Hemingway compresses the central action of the novel into three days to achieve dramatic intensity. By focusing on a mere seventy-two hours he can show us the reality of life during war in microscopic detail. He was consciously influenced by Tolstoy's *War and Peace* and managed, like Tolstoy, to communicate the broad sweep of political and military events while concentrating his narrative attention on a few fully-developed characters.

Hemingway's genius for describing beauty of place is given a powerful, ironic purpose. He makes the reader love the pine-forested hills in which the guerillas hide out, in which Jordan conducts his painfully brief affair with Maria. Yet in these same hills we are forced to witness both the bloody massacre of another guerilla gang by a Fascist patrol and the final fire-fight, in which Robert Jordan dies. The book's ominous title, the dangers of Jordan's bridge-blowing mission and Pilar's refusal to tell Jordan what she sees in his future, all contribute to the threatening atmosphere. The closeness of possible death and the lack of time intensify the love scenes between Jordan and Maria. We are forced to contemplate the almost unbearable certainty that Jordan is about to die, having just found happiness with Maria. Hemingway uses Jordan and Maria's passion as a metaphor for the Loyalist cause: their love stands for the passion and idealism of the Loyalists, a passion destroyed – in both cases – by Fascism. Every aspect of the book is characterized by artistic certainty and conviction. Inspired by his love of Spain, of Martha, of the Loyalist cause, Hemingway wrote some of his finest, simplest prose. In the following passage a Loyalist guerilla contemplates the moment of his death:

> Dying was nothing and he had no picture of it nor fear of it in his mind. But living was a field of grain blowing in the wind on the side of a hill. Living was a hawk in the sky. Living was an earthen jar of water in the dust of the threshing with the grain flailed out and the chaff blowing.

Gary Cooper and Ingrid Bergman as Robert Jordan and Maria in For Whom the Bell Tolls, *1944. The film was a box-office success.*

For Whom the Bell Tolls was published in October 1940. The film rights were sold for $100,000. A month later, Hemingway divorced Pauline and married Martha. The book had sold 785,000 copies by the end of 1943 and received excellent reviews. 'Hemingway the artist is with us again,' Edmund Wilson wrote, 'and it is like having an old friend back.' Communist commentators criticized the book because, in parts, it showed sympathy with the Fascists and disillusion with the Loyalists. Kenneth Lynn, Hemingway's most recent biographer, points out that the book expresses disillusion with politics as a whole rather than with any particular party. Lynn suggests that the book might have been titled 'Homage to Death' because, as in *Farewell to Arms*, love is sacrificed to death.

By the end of the 1930s Hemingway was reported to be drinking 17 whisky and sodas a day. His excessive intake was beginning to affect his behaviour. He and Martha argued about his lying, his untidiness (she took to calling him 'the pig') and his monstrous egotism. He hit her; she crashed his favourite car. They were living in Cuba, at the Finca Vigia, an old look-out station on a hill outside Havana. Martha had found and renovated the place and insisted on paying half the expenses.

When the USA became involved in the Second World War, Hemingway gathered some of his cronies together and, equipped with small arms, cruised the Cuban coast, supposedly gathering intelligence and hunting for submarines. It seems unlikely that Hemingway would have participated more seriously in the Second World War but for Martha's promptings. When she decided to cover the war in Europe, Hemingway landed himself the job of correspondent for the American magazine *Colliers*, a post which she would have been given under any other circumstances. He refused to help her get across to Europe. In London, he met Mary Welsh, who would become his fourth and final wife. He was frequently drunk and sustained a head injury (one of many) that landed him in hospital.

A view of the Cuban coast. During the Second World War Hemingway and some friends armed themselves and patrolled this coast, looking for enemy submarines.

The landings of Allied troops on the Normandy beaches in 1944. Recent evidence suggests that Hemingway was present as a reporter.

He was present at the Normandy landings. Recent biographers have scorned this claim as a lie but a letter published in the *Times Literary Supplement* in March 1988 from an ex-naval lieutenant firmly states that Hemingway went ashore with the troops during the first three days of the landings. If he was truly present on D-day, his reports were colourful and often wildly inaccurate. He broke the Geneva Convention, carrying and using weapons which reporters are not allowed to do. He claimed that he 'liberated' the Ritz Hotel in Paris. His water bottles were filled with hard liquor. He played the big shot, the tear-away, gathering intelligence, interrogating German prisoners, collecting a private army of adoring irregular followers around him. He was heroic in a deranged, desperate sort of way – risking his life to keep up with his myth.

He accompanied the Allied troops in the advance towards the German border. He drove a jeep through enemy occupied territory, acquired another head injury and a bad concussion which robbed him of his sexual potency. Martha, who was just as brave as her husband but did not shout about it, continued to report on the war from the front line. When they met up in Rodenbourg it was clear that their marriage was a lost cause. In Paris, Hemingway continued his courtship of Mary.

Hemingway and his friend Colonel Buck Lanham stand near a captured German gun, on the Siegfried Line. September 1944.

Hemingway writing a report on the war from London's Dorchester Hotel, in the summer of 1944.

After a drunken dinner with Marlene Dietrich and a crowd of Hemingway-loving troops he slapped Mary. She called him 'you poor, fat, feather-headed coward. You woman hitter,' and then promptly forgave him. Bill Walton, a companion at the time, recalled that Mary 'did not play up to him as a man of letters. Instead she treated him as the hotshot warrior macho man, great in bed.' Martha had been admirably independent and refused to play the little wife to the writer-hero. Mary gave Hemingway the underling's devotion that he seemed to need.

7 Humiliation and Adulation

An ageing daredevil with yet another head injury, yet another drink in hand, talks to a reporter at the Lake Victoria Hotel, Entebbe.

In the decade after the Second World War, Hemingway wrote some of his worst and one of his best books. This lack of consistency, which had been apparent to a lesser extent during the 1930s, can be blamed upon poor health, hard drinking and the depressions that these seemed to bring on. Two wartime concussions had weakened him. He suffered from various serious maladies, but had not lost his ability to enjoy himself. A.E. Hotchner, a friend he made in 1948, remarked that he 'had never seen anyone with such an aura of fun and well-being'. Others pointed out that Hemingway was seldom full of enthusiasm unless he was also full of drink.

Mary Hemingway took care of her husband as best she could and was thanked with abuse and his flirtations with other women. They spent most of their time at Finca Vigia, in Cuba, where they kept 30 cats, assorted dogs and fighting cocks. Attended by servants, Hemingway began writing – and drinking – in the early morning. As he chased his own myth of war hero, sportsman and womanizer he acted more like a fading movie star than a successful writer. Showmanship took the place of intellectual seriousness. He boasted, punched people, threw drinks in his wife's face and failed – until 1954 – to write any fiction to equal *For Whom the Bell Tolls*.

In between drinks, he poured out an enormous number of written words. He accumulated thousands of pages of a manuscript about the sea but was unable to shape this mass into a publishable work. After his death his wife and his first biographer, Carlos Baker, filleted the better sections from the manuscript and published them as *Islands in the Stream*. The book's hero, Thomas Hudson, a poorly-concealed version of Hemingway, is a painter who struggles, like his creator, to fulfil his creative potential. His failure is attended by the deaths of his three sons and one of his wives. The fates of Catherine (in *Farewell to Arms*) and Robert Jordan (in *For Whom the Bell Tolls*) have a tragic intensity which is absent from the deaths in *Islands in the Stream*. Hemingway's compulsion to kill off his characters – the

Hemingway with his fourth wife Mary on a fishing trip off Cuba.

Feeding one of the thirty cats that they kept at the Finca Vigia, in Cuba.

morbid obsession which had troubled him since his father's suicide – fails to make art. The book is divided into three sections of which the first, describing a fishing trip, is much the strongest. It would be unreasonable to condemn Hemingway for a work which he chose not to publish in his lifetime. Nonetheless, *Islands in the Stream* is sad evidence of the damage that injuries, alcohol and fame had wreaked upon him. Written by someone else it might seem promising, as a Hemingway book it seems the opposite.

The death-ridden *Islands in the Stream* seems prophetic of Hemingway's mother's death in 1951. In the same year, his second wife, Pauline, died after a row with him on the phone. Soon afterwards his editor and friend, Max Perkins, hastened to the grave. Hemingway's relationship with his mother had been characterized by conflict, and they were not on good terms when she died. His son Gregory blamed Hemingway for Pauline's death. The sense of loss and the guilt attached to these deaths brought more pressure to bear on an already troubled man.

The writer at work in his study at the Finca Vigia.

He wrote another long, unfinished manuscript during the late 1940s. It tells the story of a triangular love affair between a married couple and a young woman. The wife is mentally unstable and her disturbed personality finds its expression in sexual experimentation and envy of her husband's literary success. She destroys their marriage and burns the story on which he has been working. An edited version of the manuscript was published in 1986 as *The Garden of Eden*. The book mourns a paradise lost and hints at the guilt and remorse that Hemingway felt about his broken marriages and his apparently fading talents.

The atmosphere of destructive corruption and fevered sexuality which permeates *The Garden of Eden* is the stuff of fantasy. Hemingway involved himself in a number of fantasy relationships with young girls during his marriage to Mary. The most important of these was with Adriana Ivancich who was nineteen when he met her in 1948. She was dark-haired, Catholic, attractive but unattainable. Hemingway adored her and wrote her long, passionate letters. When Adriana came to stay in Cuba, tension mounted at the Finca, but his affair with her did not go beyond passionate friendship. He worshipped her and she was flattered. He was generous and she gave little in return.

She became the model for Renata, heroine of *Across the River and into the Trees*, published in 1950. Set in Venice, it tells the story of the ageing Colonel Richard Cantwell's love for a young Italian countess. The novel contains some fine passages, especially Hemingway's descriptions of Venice and its surrounding lagoon, but the thoughts of Cantwell, an old soldier who perceives himself as a failure, are tedious and tinged with a sickly sentimentality. The affair between Cantwell and Renata is hard to believe. Mary Hemingway saw the book's weaknesses but dared not mention them. Hemingway was shocked when the critics were less diplomatic. Cyril Conolly wrote that Cantwell is 'a drink-sodden and maundering old bore . . . His ladylove is a whimsical wax-work.'

Hemingway with Adriana Ivancich at the Finca, October 1950. Adriana was one of the young women he took to calling 'daughter'. Renata in Across the River and into the Trees *is modelled on her.*

Across the River, Islands in the Stream, and *The Garden of Eden* share the same problem. All three novels fall short of Hemingway's best because he fails to detach himself from his heroes: there is too much undigested, untransformed Hemingway in Richard Cantwell, Thomas Hudson and David Bourne. When a writer makes himself his main subject and fails to achieve any objective distance from himself, the result is often unconvincing and mawkish.

Fishing off the coast of Uganda in 1954, the year of The Old Man and the Sea.

During 1949–50, Hemingway allowed himself to be profiled by two magazines. The first piece, in *Life*, virtually disregarded Hemingway's writing and concentrated on his military and hunting exploits. Lies, inventions and rumours by and about Hemingway were set down as facts. The article fortified the Hemingway myth. In 1950, in a profile in the *New Yorker*, Hemingway confessed, 'I am a strange old man' (a phrase he later gave to Santiago, the hero of *The Old Man and the Sea*).

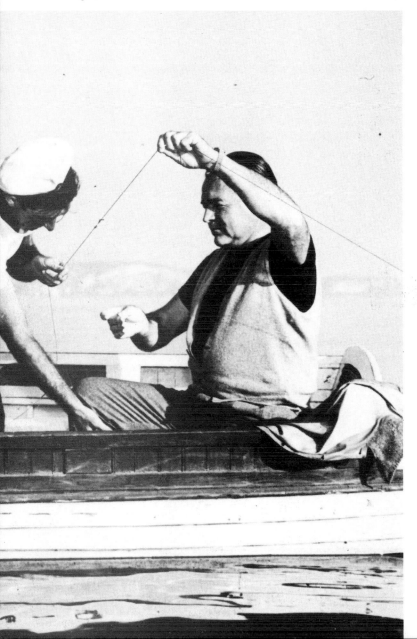

In contrast to the *Life* piece, this profile showed Hemingway as an arrogant big-shot, more fragile than heroic, trading on his past glories.

He had a habit of following a harshly criticized book with a great book, as if the determination to prove everybody wrong spurred him on to do his best work. He had reacted to a critical battering in the 1930s, by writing *For Whom the Bell Tolls*. While the critics were slamming *Across the River*, he was writing *The Old Man and the Sea*, the book which was to win him the USA's most important literary prize, the Pulitzer, when it was published in 1952.

Hemingway triumphed in *The Old Man and the Sea* because he escaped from his fantasies and his self-obsession, choosing an old Cuban fisherman, Santiago, as his hero. The tale is a parable in which the eternal struggle between man and nature is symbolized by the old man's efforts to land an enormous marlin which he hooks after 84 days of unsuccessful fishing.

Hemingway was involved for a time with the shooting of the film of The Old Man and the Sea.

Santiago and the boy, Manolin, in The Old Man and the Sea.

Hemingway had been planning the story for fifteen years; at one time it became incorporated in the *Islands in the Stream* manuscript. In it, he gathers together his slowly-accumulated knowledge of the sea, of Cuba and its fishermen, and of the marlin he had so often hunted himself. He does not display this knowledge in a flashy or boastful manner, but uses it to write a simple, compelling tale, wasting no words, using simple images:

> He was an old man who fished alone in a skiff in the Gulf Stream and he had gone eighty-four days now without taking a fish.

This sentence, which opens the book, sets the scene and establishes the uncluttered clarity of the style. The tattered sail of the old man's skiff looks like 'the flag of permanent defeat'. Santiago's essential needs are cared for by a boy, Manolin, who fished with him until his luck went bad. The old man sets out alone in search of fish. He drifts further and further from the coast. He talks to himself, missing the company of the boy.

Santiago feels one of his lines twitching. Something is eating the bait: 'This far out he must be huge in this month, he thought'. He pays out line and then holds on for dear life, the line straining to breaking point; the fish begins to tow the skiff out to sea. For hours and then days Santiago waits for the fish to tire. He knows that he must try not to 'think but only to endure'. He passes porpoises and notes that 'they are our brothers, like the flying fish'. He feels ambivalent about the vast fish he has hooked:

> His choice had been to stay in the deep dark water far out beyond all snares and traps and treacheries. My choice was to go there to find him beyond all people. Beyond all people in the world. Now we are joined together and have been since noon. And no one to help either one of us.

The old man feels a kinship with the fish but would die rather than fail in his determination to kill it. This age-old conflict between man and beast is one of Hemingway's great themes and had surfaced before in his writing about bullfighting and big-game hunting. Santiago begins to think of the great fish as his brother, just as Pedro Romero, in *Fiesta*, thought of the bulls he was about to kill as his friends.

Santiago endures pain and exhaustion and the 'humiliation' of cramps in his hand. He forces himself to eat raw fish.

> Then he was sorry for the great fish that had nothing to eat and his determination to kill him never relaxed in his sorrow for him.

On the second night of the struggle, the old man fixes his line so that he can sleep. He wakes to find that the final fight has started: the fish has come to the surface. After a long battle in which the old man almost loses consciousness due to exhaustion and pain, he harpoons and kills the fish. He has to lash the marlin to the side of the skiff because it is too big to take on board. As the old man sails for home with his mighty catch, sharks, attracted by the scent of blood, attack the dead marlin. The old man kills shark after shark until his harpoon, his knife and his club are all lost.

After the shark attack the old man says to himself, 'A man can be destroyed but not defeated', and it is this stoicism that is central to the meaning of *The Old Man and the Sea*. The great marlin stands for all men's crowning ambitions; ambitions which can sometimes only be achieved (like Macbeth's, for example) at the price of

Spencer Tracy as Santiago battles with the fish in The Old Man and the Sea.

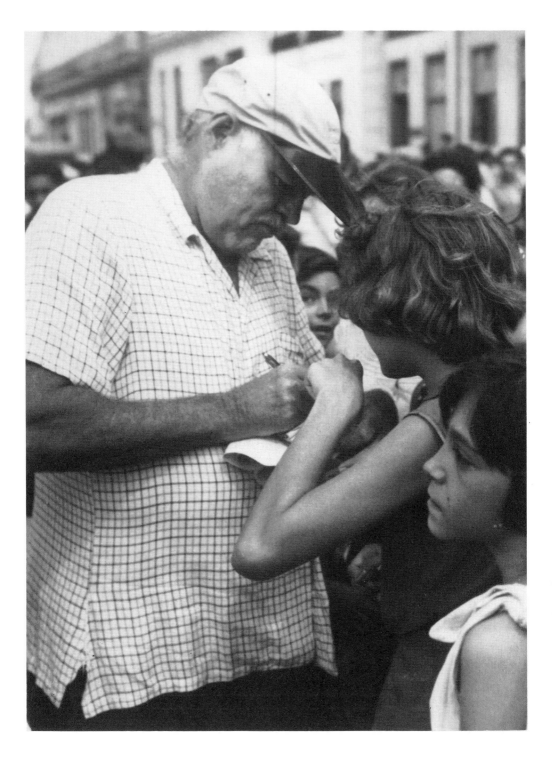

destruction. The old man survives his ordeal, undefeated. Again and again he overcomes his pain and fatigue:

> He took all his pain and what was left of his strength and his long-gone pride and he put it against the fish's agony . . .

Perhaps the heart of the story's capacity to move its readers is in Hemingway's exploration of the bond between man and nature. The old man loves that which he seeks to kill. He depends upon the sea and its fish for his livelihood and kills that which he depends upon. This paradoxical truth – that we love the world and yet destroy its creatures for our own survival – is a longstanding literary theme. The bond between the old man and the fish is symbolized by the line that joins them throughout their struggle. The old man has the simple wisdom to understand that there is no true conflict between his love for the marlin and his determination to kill it. When the sharks destroy the marlin he feels remorse for what he has done, because the marlin's dignity has been lost:

> I wish it were a dream and that I had never hooked him. I'm sorry about it, fish. It makes everything wrong.

The fish is the image of the man's triumph over nature; when the fish is mutilated this triumph is compromised:

> He did not like to look at the fish any more since he had been mutilated. When the fish had been hit it was as though he himself had been hit.

With the publication of *The Old Man and the Sea* Hemingway's literary stock enjoyed its last and biggest rise. The whole story was published in *Life* magazine and sold over five million copies in two days. Hemingway scholars now find it fashionable to criticize *The Old Man and the Sea*, identifying in it the self-pity and bogus sentimentality that weakened much of the rest of his work of the period. Yet the reviewers of the time were almost unanimous in finding it Hemingway's greatest work. Cyril Conolly, who had been so dismissive of *Across the River* wrote, 'I believe it is one of the best stories Hemingway has ever written'.

Opposite
Hemingway signing autographs during the filming of The Old Man and the Sea.

In 1953 to 1954, the Hemingways undertook a second African safari. Ernest drank heavily and shot inaccurately. The trip produced some mediocre essays but no fiction. Almost as if his myth were taking revenge upon him, he was involved in two plane crashes in three days. He and Mary both suffered injuries, Hemingway's being yet another concussion. After the first accident the couple were believed dead and the world's press issued obituaries which Hemingway read with fascination. He had survived his own public death but his health was again weakened. While helping to extinguish a forest fire soon after the plane crashes he was badly burnt. His friend A.E. Hotchner noted that 'some of the aura of massiveness seemed to have gone out of him'.

While he was making news in Africa, Hemingway was awarded the Nobel prize for literature. He did not collect the award in person but wrote a candid, dignified acceptance speech:

Writing, at its best, is a lonely life. Organizations for writers palliate the writer's loneliness but I doubt if they improve his writing. He grows in public stature as he sheds his loneliness and often his work deteriorates. For he does his work alone and if he is a good enough writer he must face eternity, or the lack of it, each day.

8 Despair and Suicide

Hemingway never fully recovered from his African injuries. New health problems emerged – hypertension, chronic liver malfunction – but worse than these was the decline in his mental health. He became increasingly testy, argumentative, suspicious and guilt-ridden. He worked on his African journals but did not write anything he considered worth publishing. He was involved in the filming of *The Old Man and the Sea*, which starred Spencer Tracy as Santiago.

In 1957, he learnt of the existence of two forgotten trunks which had been sitting in the cellars of the Paris Ritz since 1928. Using the mementoes and notebooks that he recovered from these trunks, he began work on *A Moveable Feast*, his fictionalized autobiography of his formative, happy years in Paris in the 1920s. Writing about this golden past gave him some relief from the harsh present of his ailing body and wavering mind. *A Moveable Feast* was published after his death in 1964 and provides valuable information about the Paris years, spiced with some characteristically tall stories. Vicious portraits of men like Scott Fitzgerald, Ford Madox Ford and Wyndham Lewis with whom Hemingway had fallen out, are combined with descriptions of poverty and artistic struggle told in a romanticized but nonetheless touching fashion.

In 1959, Hemingway revisited Spain, commissioned to write about the rivalry between two great bullfighters. He celebrated his sixtieth birthday in Malaga and exhausted himself by trailing the bullfighters across Spain. The record of this trip, published posthumously

Opposite *On the library steps at the Finca Vigia, late 1950s.*

as *The Dangerous Summer*, is Hemingway's last salute to Spain and bullfighting. While trying to bring the bulging manuscript of *The Dangerous Summer* under control, he confided to his friend A.E. Hotchner, 'I'll tell you, Hotch, it is like being in a Kafka nightmare. I can act cheerful like always but am not. I'm bone tired and very beat-up emotionally.' He was tortured by insomnia, loneliness and waves of remorse about his past

During the last trip to Spain (for The **Dangerous Summer***) Hemingway salutes the great bullfighter Antonio Ordonez, in Madrid. Ordonez dedicated his bull to Hemingway.*

behaviour. He had become paranoid and believed that the 'feds' (Federal Bureau of Investigation) were after him. Although comfortably affluent he developed an irrational fear of poverty and a great dread of infringing the law.

Political tension in Cuba had forced him to move to Ketchum, Idaho, where he bought a suitably bleak house. He became more obviously disturbed, acting out

suicide before gatherings of friends. On one occasion he and Mary threatened each other with guns.

He was persuaded to enter the Mayo Clinic in Rochester, Minnesota, where a doctor prescribed electric shock treatment for his depression. It is generally agreed that the clinic made mistakes in treating Hemingway. After the shock treatment he found that his memory had more or less deserted him. He felt blank and empty. Final defeat came when, asked to write a sentence for an inaugural volume for John F. Kennedy in 1961, he was unable, after a day's struggle, to produce a single word. When the doctor arrived, Hemingway broke down and wept. 'It just won't come any more'. He returned to the Mayo, quickly convinced his doctors that he had recovered and, to Mary's alarm, returned home. On Sunday 2 July 1961, early in the morning, he shot himself through the head with a double-barrelled shotgun.

Hemingway with his last wife, Mary, at his last home, in Ketchum, Idaho, 1959.

The bleak house in Ketchum, Idaho where Hemingway spent his last days. The twisted vegetation in the foreground seems to suggest the emotional torment of Hemingway's last years.

Hemingway had come to stand for the tough approach to pain and suffering. He represented a heroic determination to experience and survive accidents, wars and calamities of all sorts. His suicide seemed to deny the validity of the legend about his life. One of the most perceptive comments about Hemingway's significance comes from the novelist Norman Mailer:

> It is not likely that Hemingway was a brave man who sought danger for the sake of the sensations it provided him. What is more likely the truth of his own odyssey is that he struggled with his cowardice and against a secret lust to suicide all his life, that his inner landscape was a nightmare, and he spent his nights wrestling with the gods. It may even be that the final judgement on his work may come to the notion that what he failed to do was tragic, but what he accomplished was heroic, for it is possible that he carried a weight of anxiety with him which would have suffocated any man smaller than himself.

The distinctive prose style that Hemingway developed and refined in the 1920s was a gift to the world which, on its own, would have justified his life. His love of the earth and his capacity to convey that love in clear, memorable words and images is not diminished by the fact of his suicide. It is tragic that a man who loved the world so much should choose to hasten his exit from it. His gift as a writer was at the heart of Hemingway's life – without it his world was colourless.

When he was nineteen, Hemingway wrote, 'How much better to die in all the happy period of undisillusioned youth, to go out in a blaze of light, than to have your body worn out and old and illusions shattered.' Perhaps Hemingway's greatest act of courage was to live on as long as he did through the years of lost illusions.

The Daily Express *front page on the day after Hemingway's death by suicide, July 1961.*

Opposite
Hemingway in the woods near his home in 1961, the year he died. This photograph suggests the loneliness of a man who had once been surrounded by friends.

Glossary

Aesthetic Concerned with the beautiful, with artistic sense and taste.

Adulation Exaggerated praise.

Alienation Estrangement, feeling of remoteness.

American Civil War 1860–65, between the northern and southern states. The North fought to end slavery in the South.

Ambivalent Feeling two different things at once.

Anecdote Short account describing an event.

Characterization The creation of fictional characters.

Communism Political belief that all property and wealth should be shared equally.

Conrad, Joseph Polish-born novelist who wrote in English. His *Heart of Darkness* (1902), is one of the great novellas of the century.

Cub-reporter Apprentice working on a newspaper.

De Maupassant, Guy French nineteenth-century writer, master of the short story form.

Dogmatic Opinionated.

Egotism Selfishness.

Eulogy A piece of writing praising something.

Expatriate Someone who lives in a country other than that of their birth.

Fascism Authoritarian, right-wing political belief.

Flawed Faulty, defective.

Genoa Conference International Economic Conference, held in Genoa, Italy, in 1922.

Greco–Turkish War 1920–22, won by the Turks.

House style The manner of writing particular to a magazine.

Imagery The verbal pictures with which writers convey their meaning.

Impotence Inability to perform sexually.

Inaugurate Begin.

Indomitable Unbeatable.

Irony A form of expression in which the intended meaning is the opposite of the words used.

Intertwined Woven together.

Lausanne Conference International Economic Conference, held in Switzerland in 1922.

Modernism A movement amongst writers and painters during 1910–25. The Modernists rejected traditional styles and subjects, determined to 'make it new'.

Morbid Preoccupied with death.

Moveable Feast A religious holiday, like Easter, which falls on a different date each year.

Mussolini, Benito Fascist dictator who led Italy into the Second World War.

Narrative Story, account.

Normandy landings On 6 June 1944 (D–Day) Allied forces began the liberation of Western Europe from the Germans by landing on the Normandy coast of France. After heavy fighting in Normandy, troops penetrated the interior and liberated Paris on 25 August and Brussels on 2 September.

Parable Story that illustrates a moral point.

Paradox Something that appears self-contradictory.

Parody Mocking imitation of another writer's style.

Platonic affair A sexually unconsummated relationship.

Pimp One who arranges sexual liaisons between people.

Posthumous After death.

Precipitate Bring about.

Rhetorical Elegant and flourishing (rhetoric = [literally] the language of persuasion).

Satire An exaggerated, mocking style that forms a moral commentary on its subject.

Shock-troops Highly-trained, assault infantry.

Symbolize Stand for, represent.

Tolstoy, Leo Russian nineteenth-century novelist. His *War and Peace* was one of the books that influenced Hemingway.

Tour de force Powerful display.

Turgenev, Ivan Russian nineteenth-century writer. His *Sportsman's Sketches* contributed to Hemingway's skill in describing countryside.

Unanimous All of the same opinion.

Vignette A brief description or small portrait.

List of Dates

1899	21 July: Born Oak Park, Chicago.
1917	Joins staff of *Kansas City Star*.
1918	Wounded while working for the Red Cross in Italy.
1920	Marries Hadley Richardson. Moves to Paris.
1923	First son born. Publishes *Three Stories and Ten Poems*.
1924	*in our time*.
1925	*In Our Time*.
1926	*The Torrents of Spring*. *The Sun Also Rises* (published in Britain as *Fiesta*).
1927	Divorces Hadley and publishes *Men Without Women*.
1928	Marries Pauline Pfeiffer and moves to Key West, Florida. His father commits suicide.
1929	Publishes *A Farewell to Arms*.
1932	*Death in the Afternoon*.
1933	*Winner Takes Nothing*.
1934	First African safari.
1935	*Green Hills of Africa*.
1937	*To Have and Have Not*. Visits Spain as journalist during the Civil War.
1938	Publishes his only play, *The Fifth Column*.
1940	Marries Martha Gellhorn and publishes *For Whom the Bell Tolls*.
1944	Reports as a war correspondent from Europe. Participates in the Normandy landings.
1945	Divorces Martha. Works on what would become *Islands in the Stream* (published posthumously in 1970).
1946	Marries Mary Welsh. Works on what would become *The Garden of Eden* (published posthumously in 1986).
1950	Publishes *Across the River and into the Trees*.
1951	His mother and his second wife both die.
1952	*The Old Man and the Sea*.

1953	Wins the Pulitzer Prize.
1954	Awarded the Nobel Prize for Literature. Second African Safari.
1958–60	Works on *The Dangerous Summer* (published posthumously in 1985) and on *A Moveable Feast* (published posthumously in 1964).
1961	2 July: Commits suicide.

Further Reading

Books by Hemingway
All Hemingway's books from 1926 onwards are available in paperback, published by Grafton. The collection of stories first published in 1925 as *In Our Time* is now entitled *The Snows of Kilimanjaro* and opens with the story of that name.

Biography and criticism
BAKER, CARLOS *Ernest Hemingway: a Life Story* (Penguin, 1987)
BRIAN, DENNIS *The Faces of Hemingway* (Grafton, 1988)
BRUCCOLI, MATTHEW *Scott and Ernest* (Random House, 1978)
BURGESS, ANTONY *Ernest Hemingway* (Thames & Hudson, 1978)
FENTON, CHARLES A. *The Apprenticeship of Ernest Hemingway* (Plantin paperbacks, 1987)
GRIFFIN, PETER *Along with Youth* (O.U.P., 1985)
KERT, BERNICE *The Hemingway Women* (Norton, 1984)
LYNN, KENNETH S. *Hemingway* (Simon & Schuster, 1987)
MEYERS, JEFFREY *Ernest Hemingway: a Biography*, (Paladin, 1986)
MEYERS, JEFFREY *Hemingway: the Critical Heritage*, (RKP, 1982)
PHILLIPS, LARRY (ed) *Hemingway on Writing* (Grafton, 1985)
REYNOLDS, MICHAEL *The Young Hemingway* (Blackwell, 1986)
REYNOLDS, MICHAEL *Hemingway's First War* (Blackwell, 1987)
ROSS, LILLIAN *Portrait of Hemingway* (Simon & Schuster, 1961)

Index

Picture acknowledgements

The author and publishers would like to thank the following for allowing their illustrations to be reproduced in this book: BBC Hulton Picture Library 7, 8, 9, 26, 27, 30, 31, 33, 44, 50–51, 59, 71, 72, 73, 74, 77, 78, 86–7; the Sylvia Beach Collection at Princeton University 28–9; John Frost Historical Newspaper Service 103; the Hemingway Collection, John F. Kennedy Library 10–11, 12, 13, 14, 16, 18, 20, 21, 22–3, 25, 38–9, 43, 46, 53, 58, 61, 63, 64, 65, 66–7, 69, 79, 80, 82, 83, 85, 94, 97, 101, 102; the National Film Archive 56, 76, 88, 89, 91, 92; Topham Picture Library 34, 36, 41, 49, 55, 62, 81, 84, 98–9, 100. All other pictures are from the Wayland Picture Library.